STARTERS NATURE

Look at Leaves

Macdonald Educational

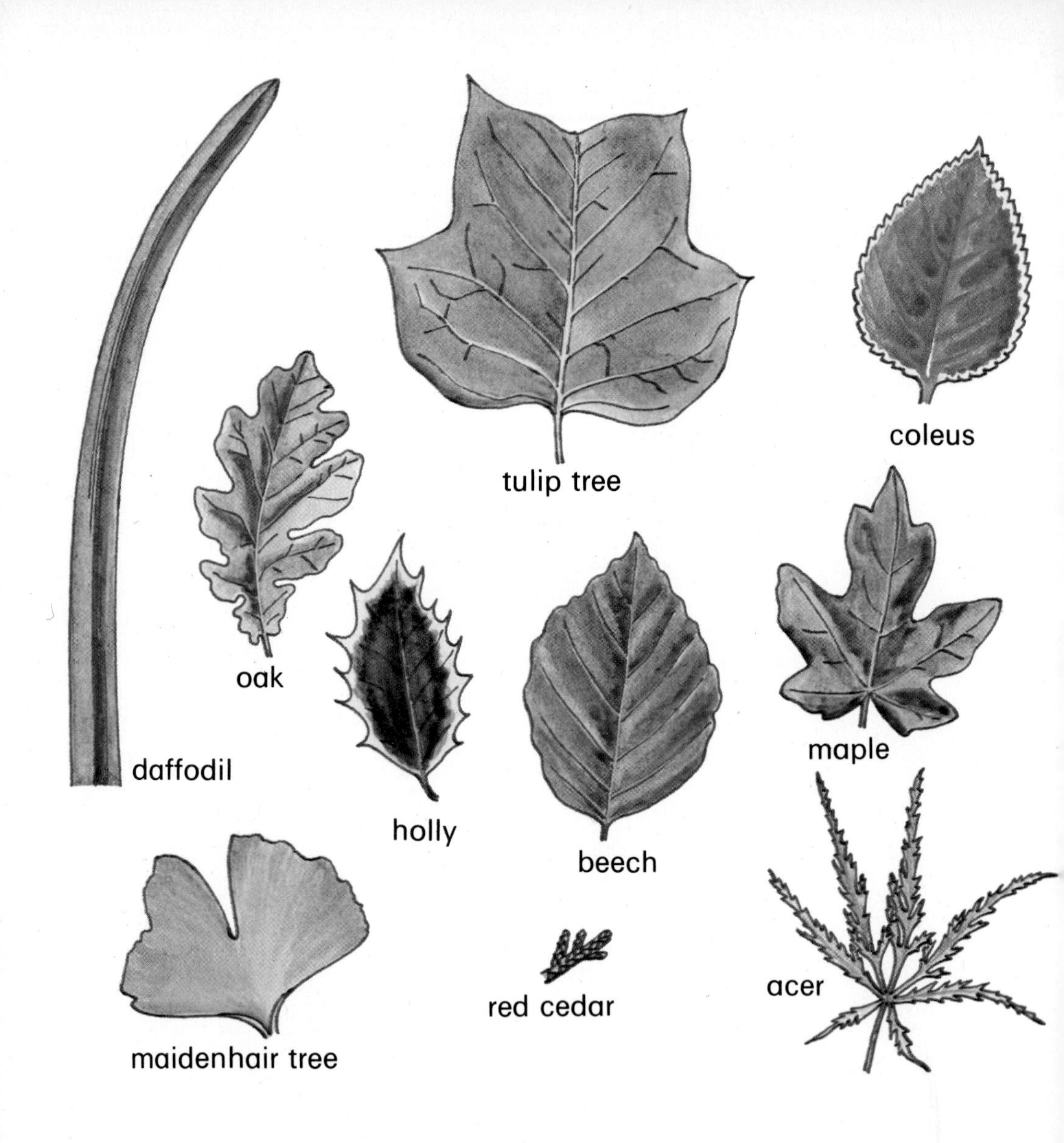
tulip tree
coleus
oak
daffodil
holly
beech
maple
maidenhair tree
red cedar
acer

There are very many different leaves.
Collect them from trees, bushes
and other plants.

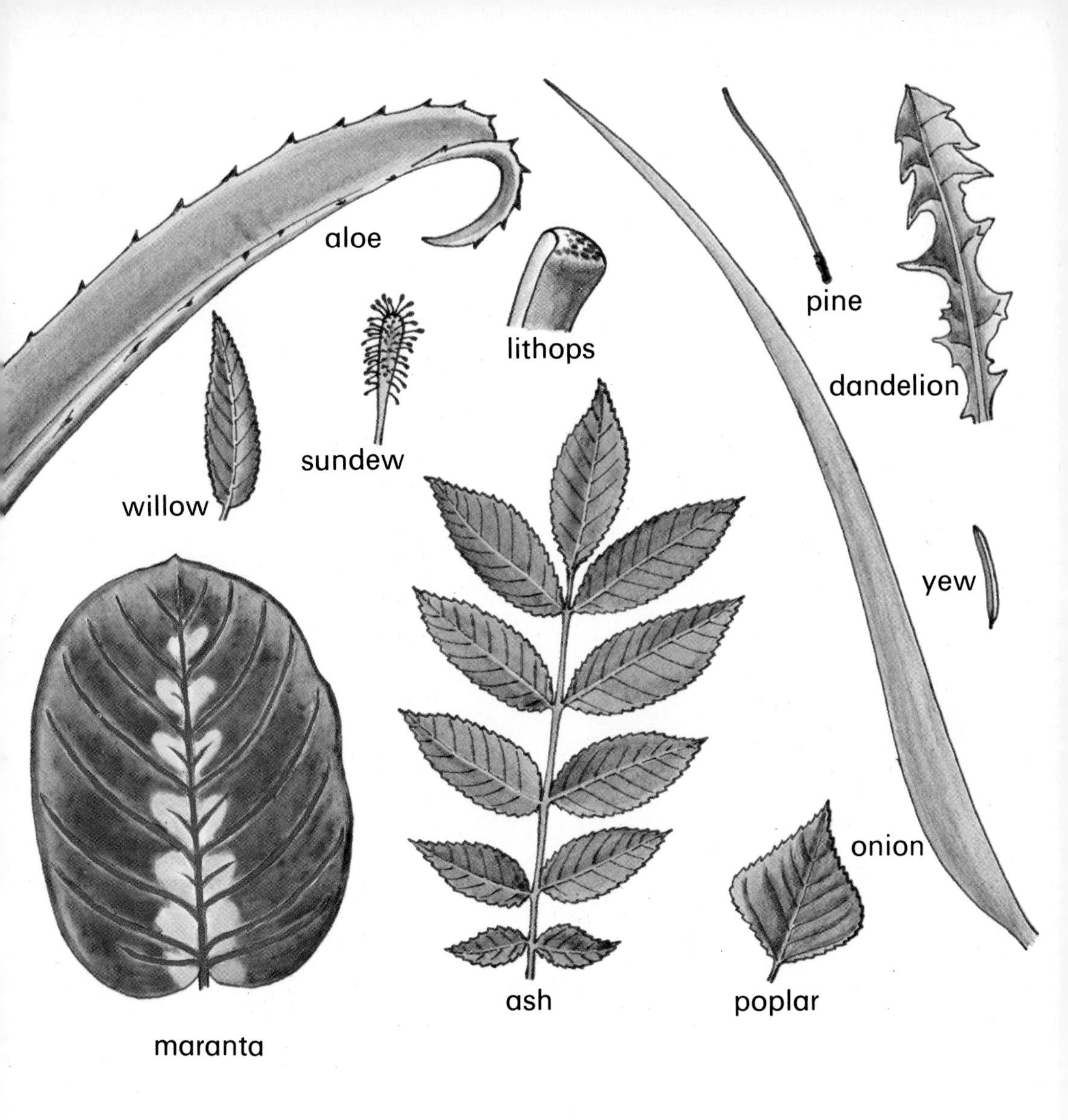
aloe
pine
lithops
dandelion
sundew
willow
yew
onion
ash
poplar
maranta

How many different shapes can you find?
How many different colours?
Label each leaf with its name.

box
rhubarb
dock
Scots pine
horse
chestnut
moss
heather

Which is the smallest leaf you can find?
Which is the biggest?

These huge water lilies
grow in South America.
They are 2 metres across.

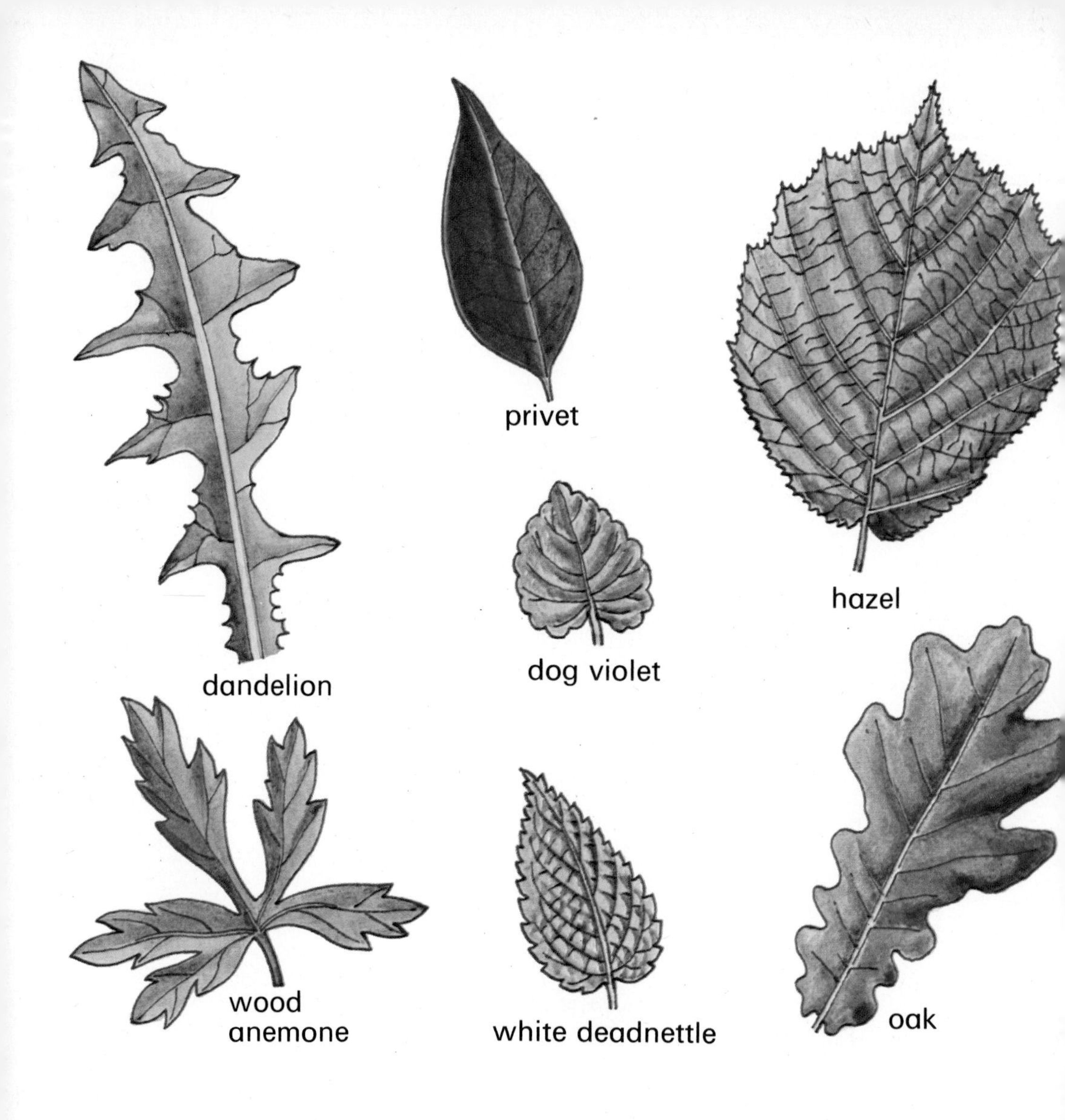
privet
hazel
dandelion
dog violet
wood
anemone
white deadnettle
oak

Look at the edges of leaves.
Can you find some of these kinds?

holly

thistle

The edges of these leaves
are very prickly.

comfrey
goose-grass
hedge
woundwort

Some leaves have hairs on them.
Some hairy leaves feel rough.
Others feel smooth.
See which you can find.

stinging
hairs

Nettles are covered with hairs.
Some hairs are long, some are short.
The long ones sting.
Look at nettle leaves with a magnifier.

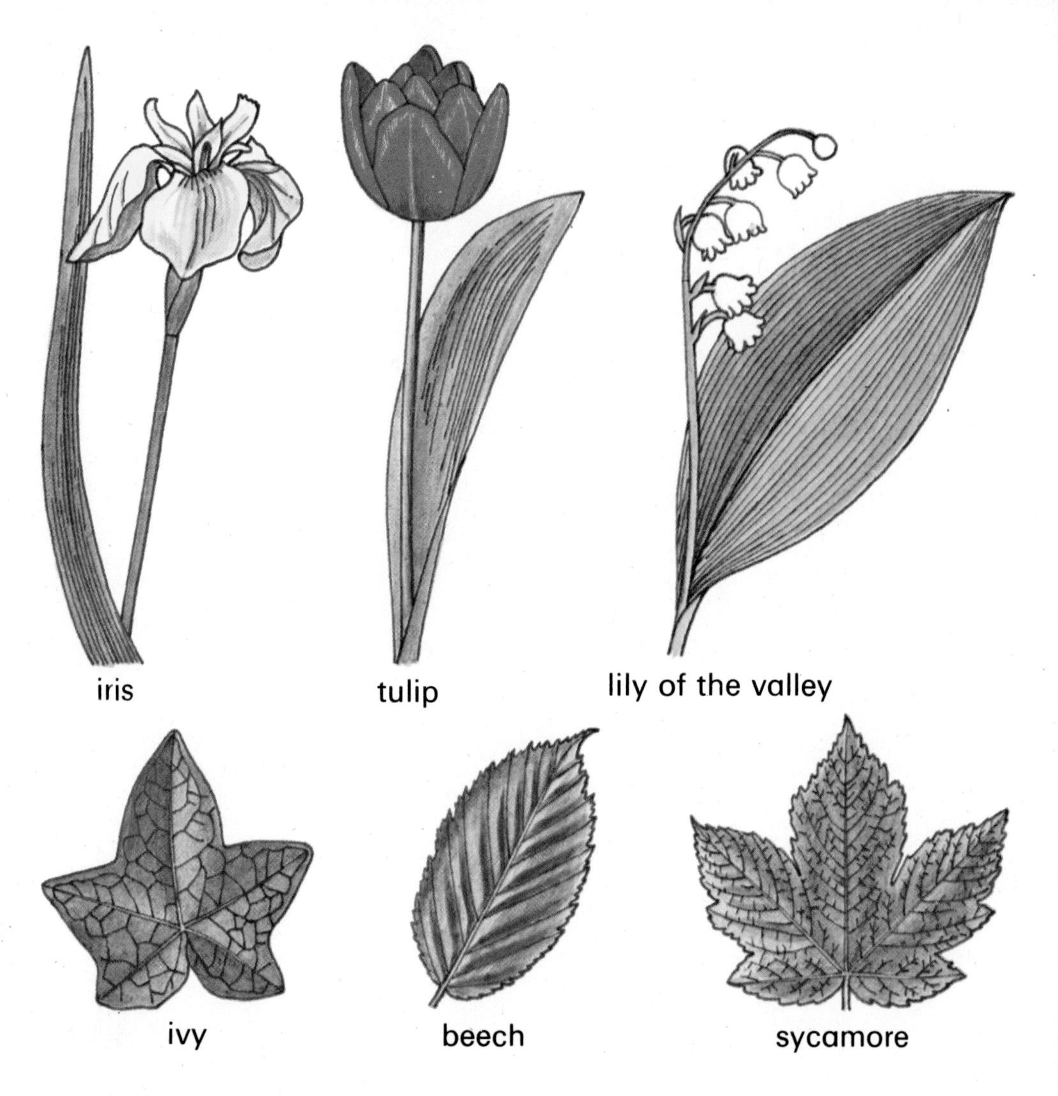
iris
tulip
lily of the valley
ivy
beech
sycamore

Look for the veins in leaves.
Some are long and straight.
Some divide into branches.
Find some of each kind.

ash
horse chestnut
elder
rose

Some leaves are made up of several leaflets.
Together these make the complete leaf.
How many of this kind can you find?

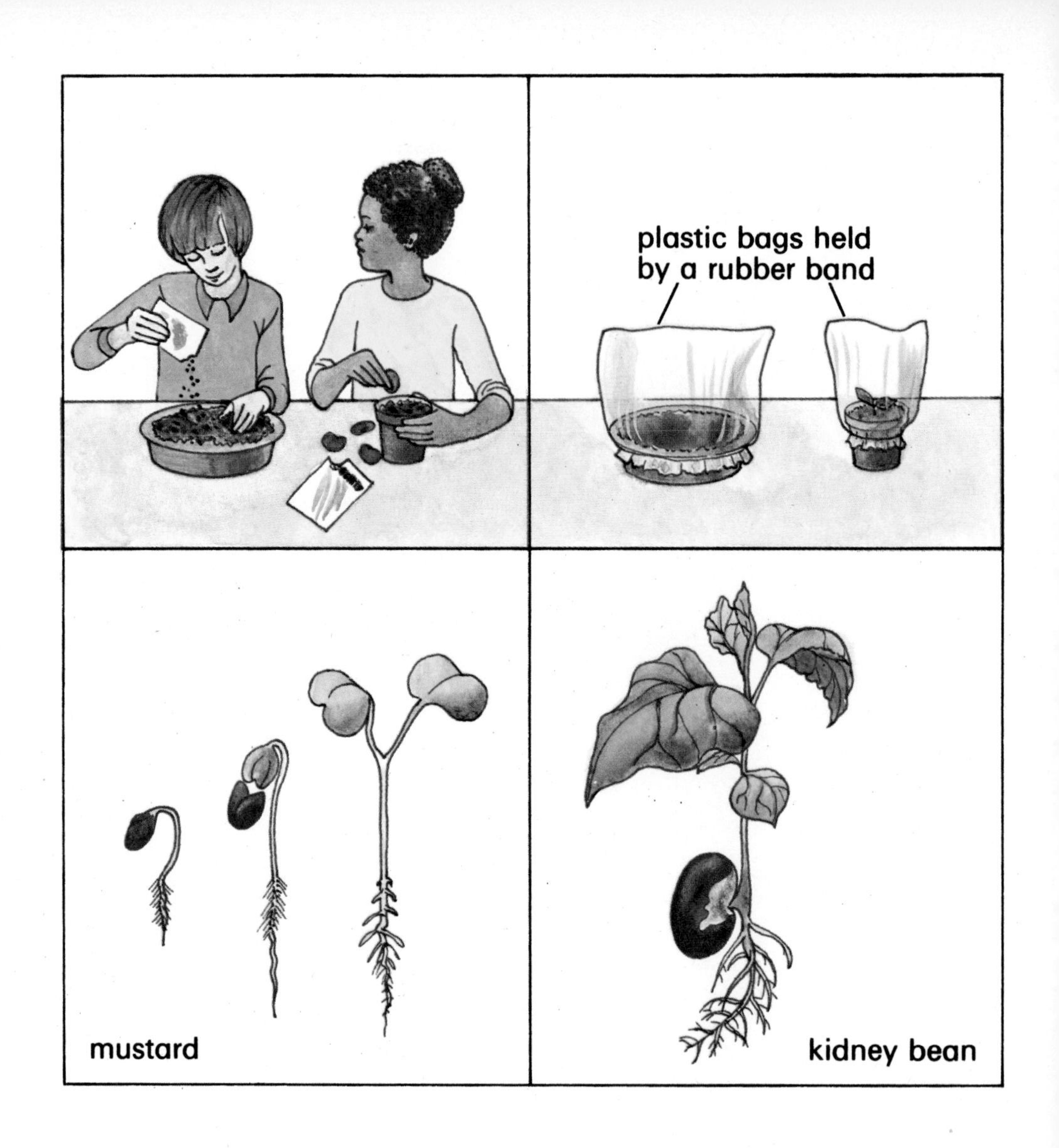
plastic bags held
by a rubber band
mustard
kidney bean

Grow some seeds.
Watch how the leaves unfold.

beech
horse chestnut
horse
chestnut
beech

In early spring, collect some twigs.
Keep them in water.
Watch the leaves grow from the buds.

rosemary
onion
thyme
spearmint
basil
tansy
chives
parsley

Pinch these leaves.
Then smell them.
They all have a strong scent.
Try many other leaves.

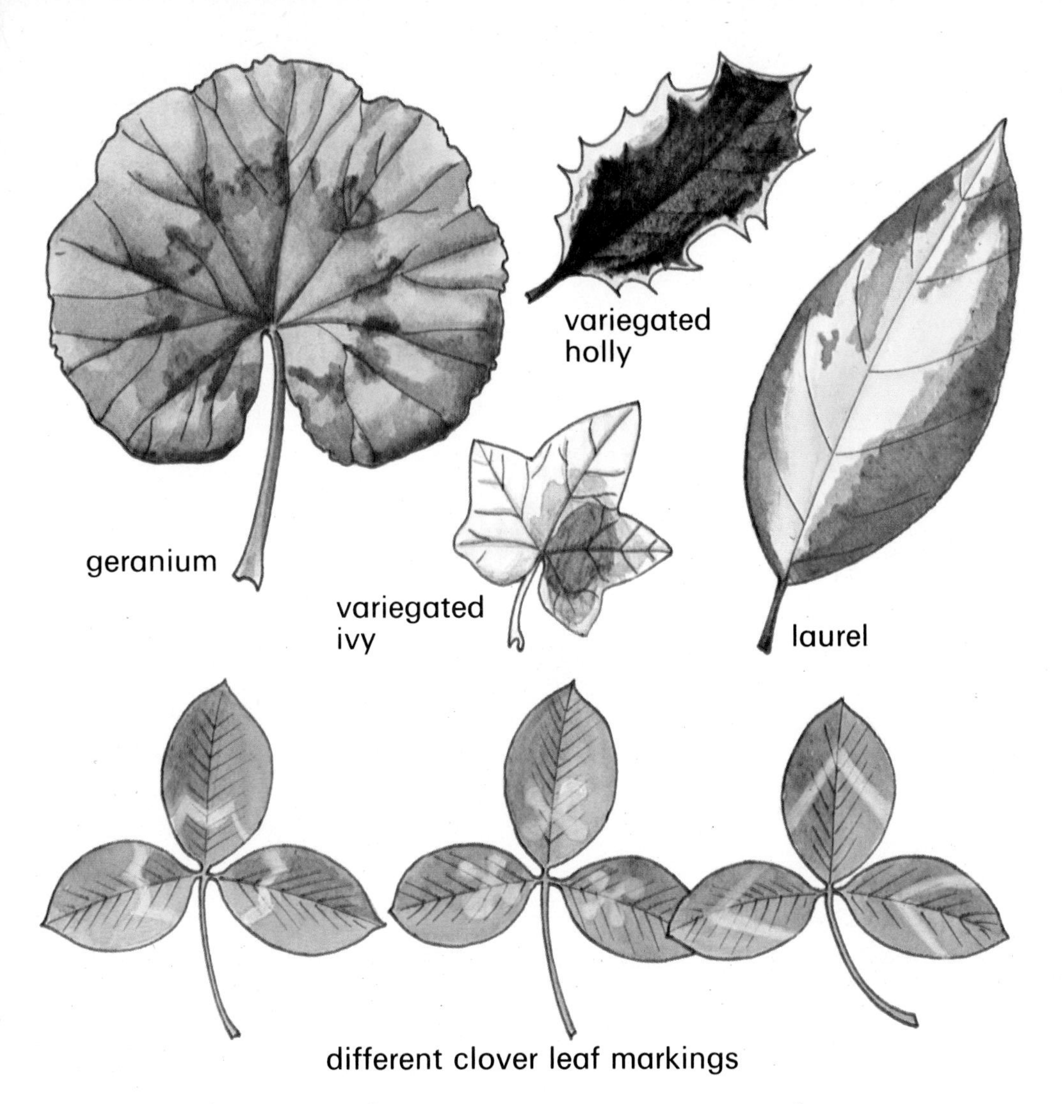
variegated
holly
geranium
variegated
ivy
laurel

different clover leaf markings

These leaves have patterns on them.
Look for leaves like these.
How many different markings
can you find on clover leaves?

People grow these plants in pots.
Many of them have interesting leaves.
They are often kept in rooms.

giraffe
koala bear

Many animals eat leaves.
Koala bears eat eucalyptus leaves.
Giraffes can reach the leaves
at the top of shrubs and trees.

sheep
cows
horses
haymaking

Cows, sheep and horses eat grass leaves.
Grass is dried to make hay
for them to eat in winter.

What animals are eating these leaves?
What other leaves do they eat?
Look for other leaves with holes in them.
Try to find out what is making the holes.

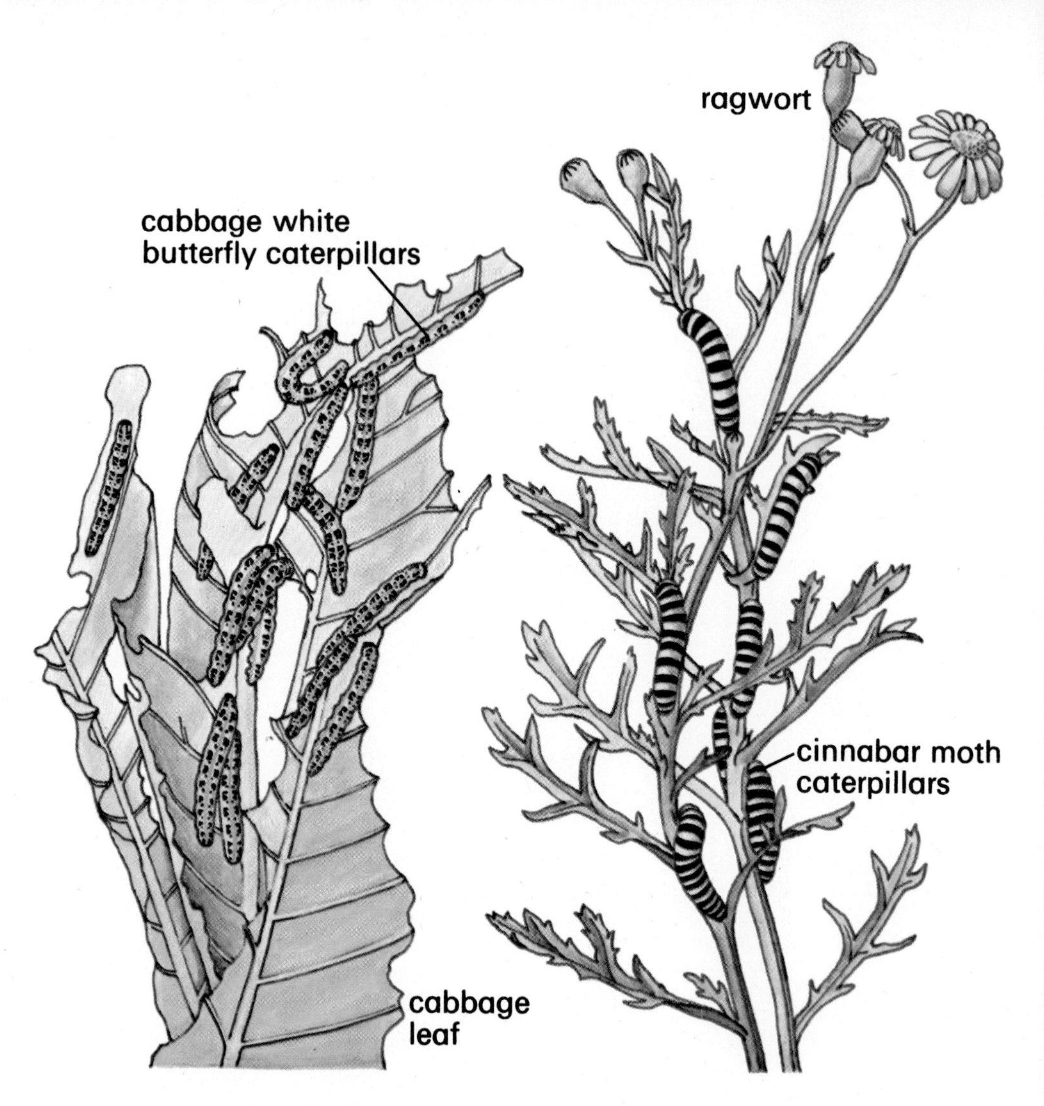
ragwort
cabbage white
butterfly caterpillars
cinnabar moth
caterpillars
cabbage
leaf

Caterpillars eat leaves.
Each kind of caterpillar
has its own food plant.
It will not eat anything else.

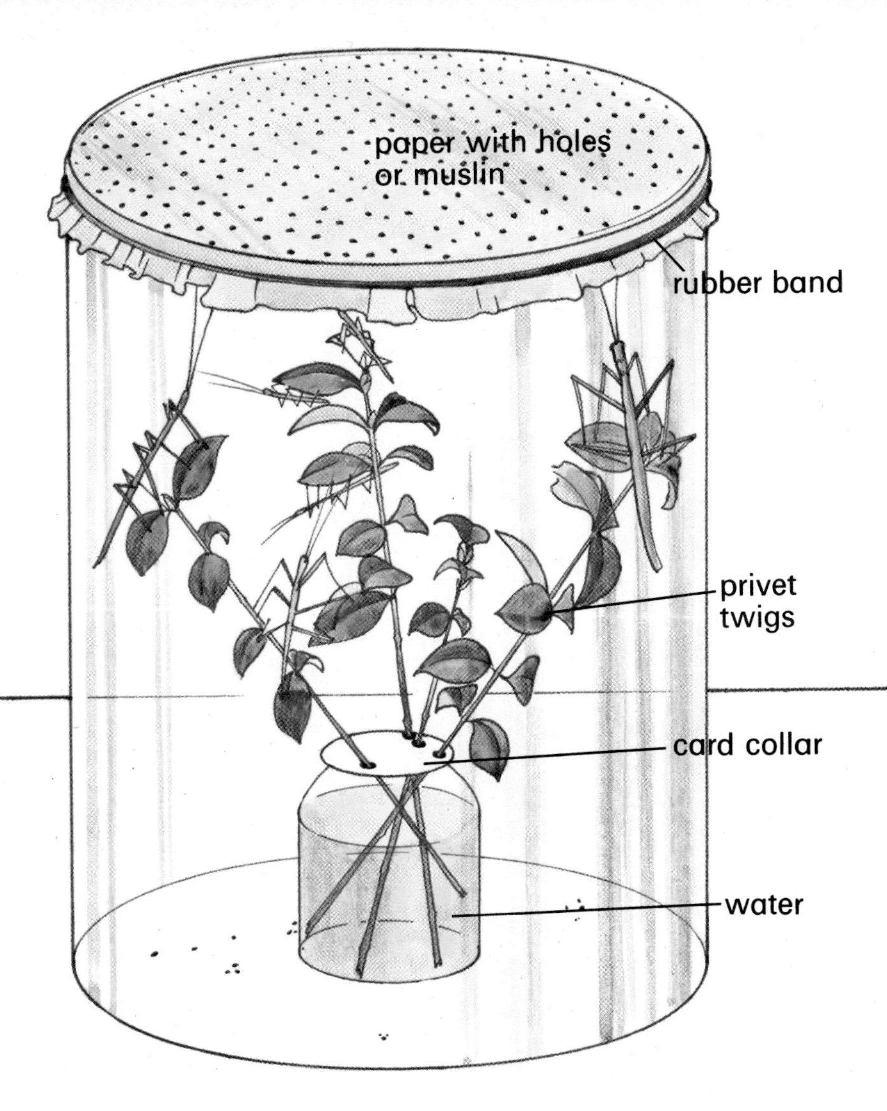
paper with holes
or muslin
rubber band
privet
twigs
card collar
water

How many stick insects can you see?
They eat privet leaves.
You can keep them in large jars.
Make small holes in the lids for air.

mustard
and
cress
Brussels
sprouts
cos lettuces
lettuces
chives
cauliflowers
spinach
red cabbages
green cabbages

These are some leaves that we eat.

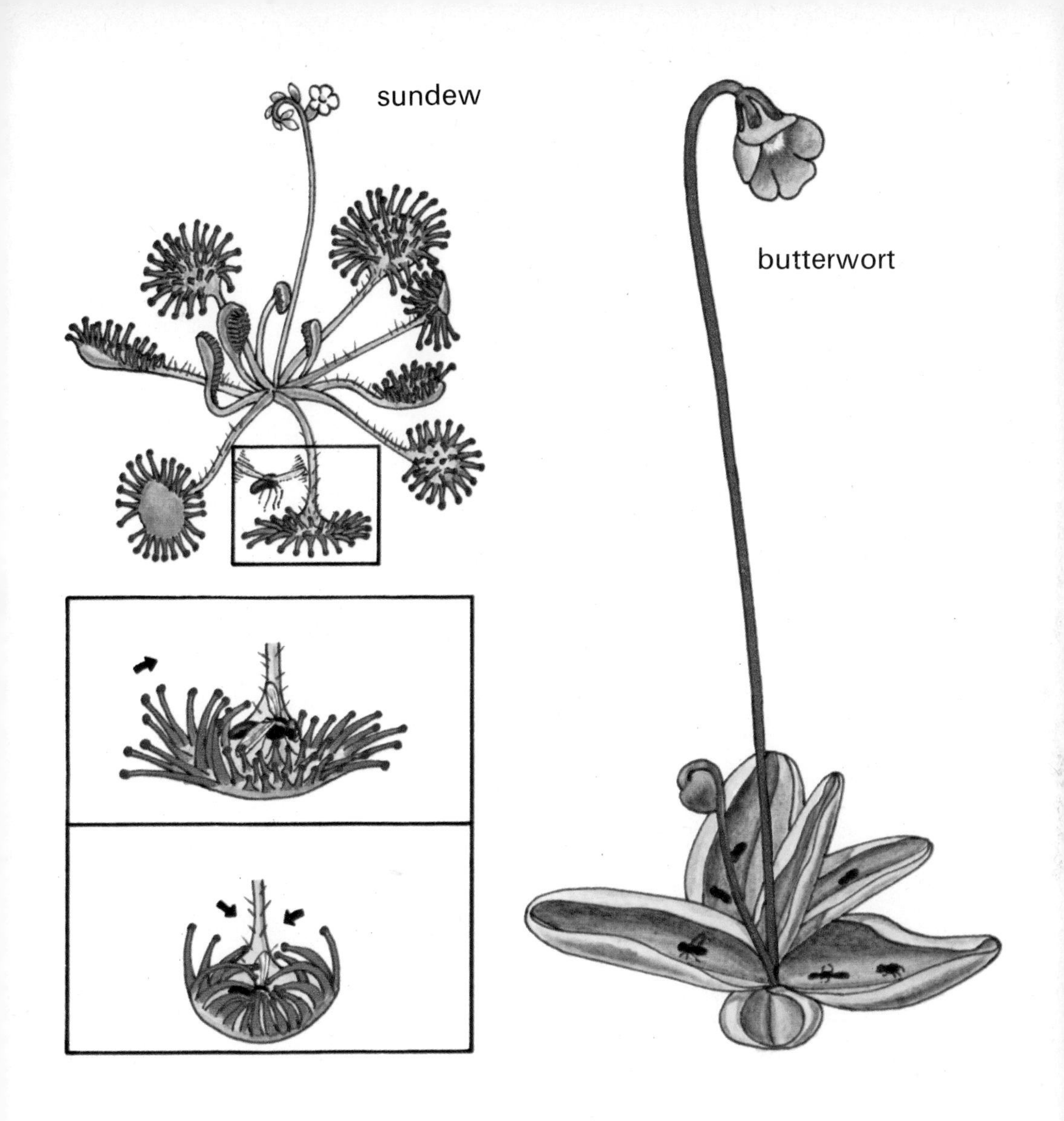
sundew
butterwort

These two plants trap insects. Their sticky leaves catch them and then dissolve them.

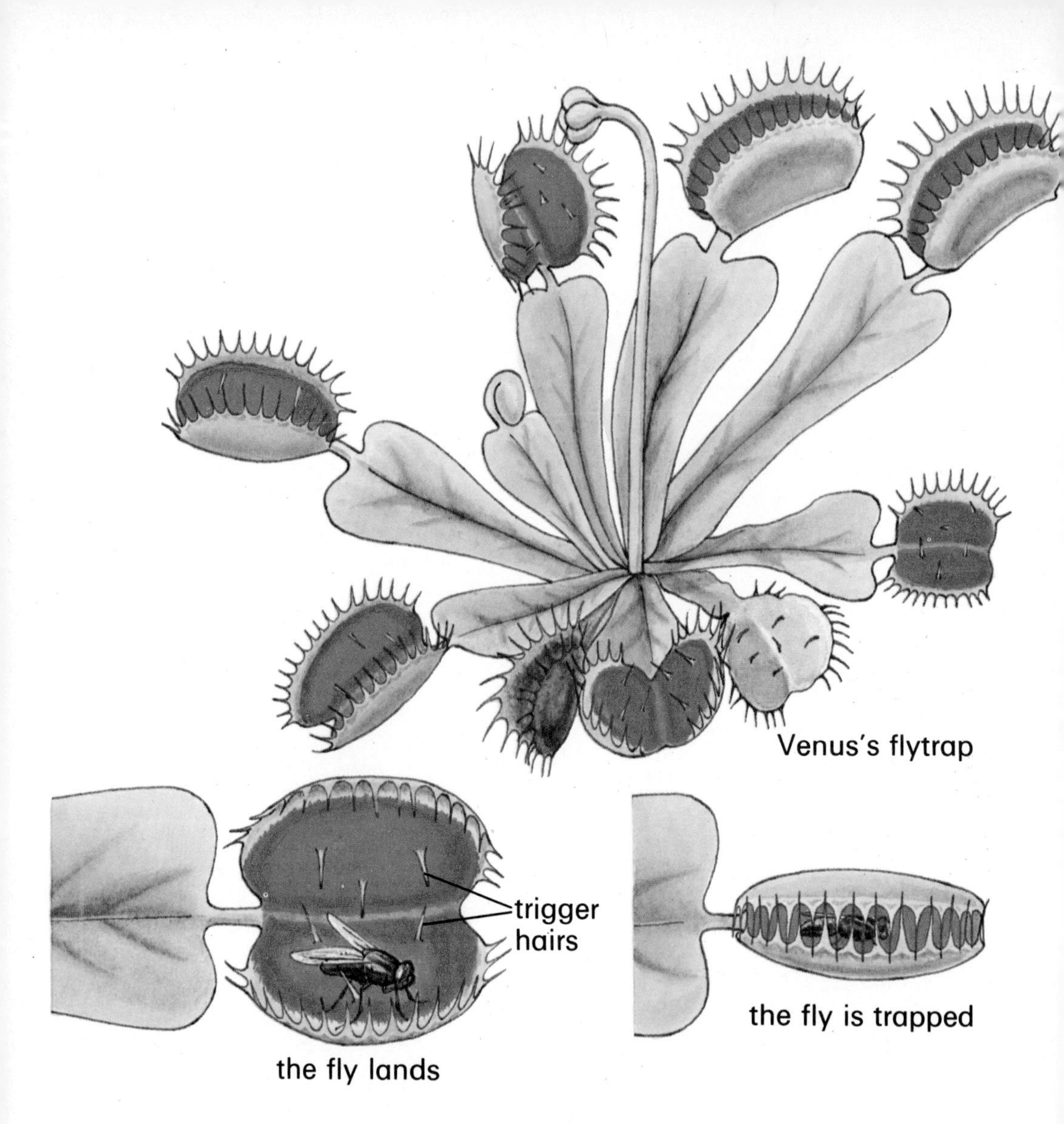
Venus's flytrap
trigger
hairs
the fly is trapped
the fly lands

The leaf of this plant is a trap.
If an insect touches the trigger hairs,
the two parts close together quickly.

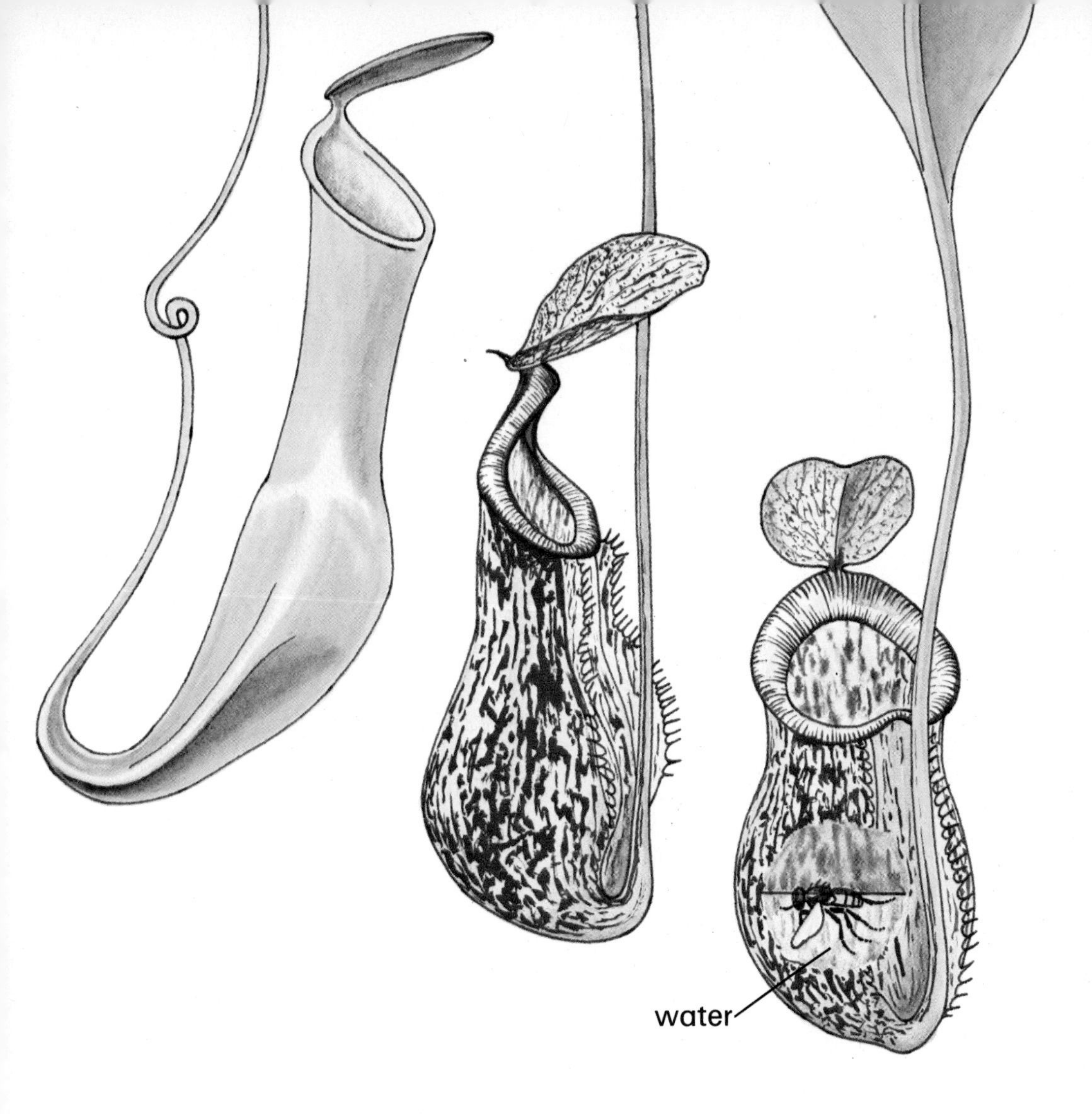
water

These plants grow in hot countries.
The pitcher shape is on the end of the leaf.
It has water in it.
Insects fall in, drown and are digested.

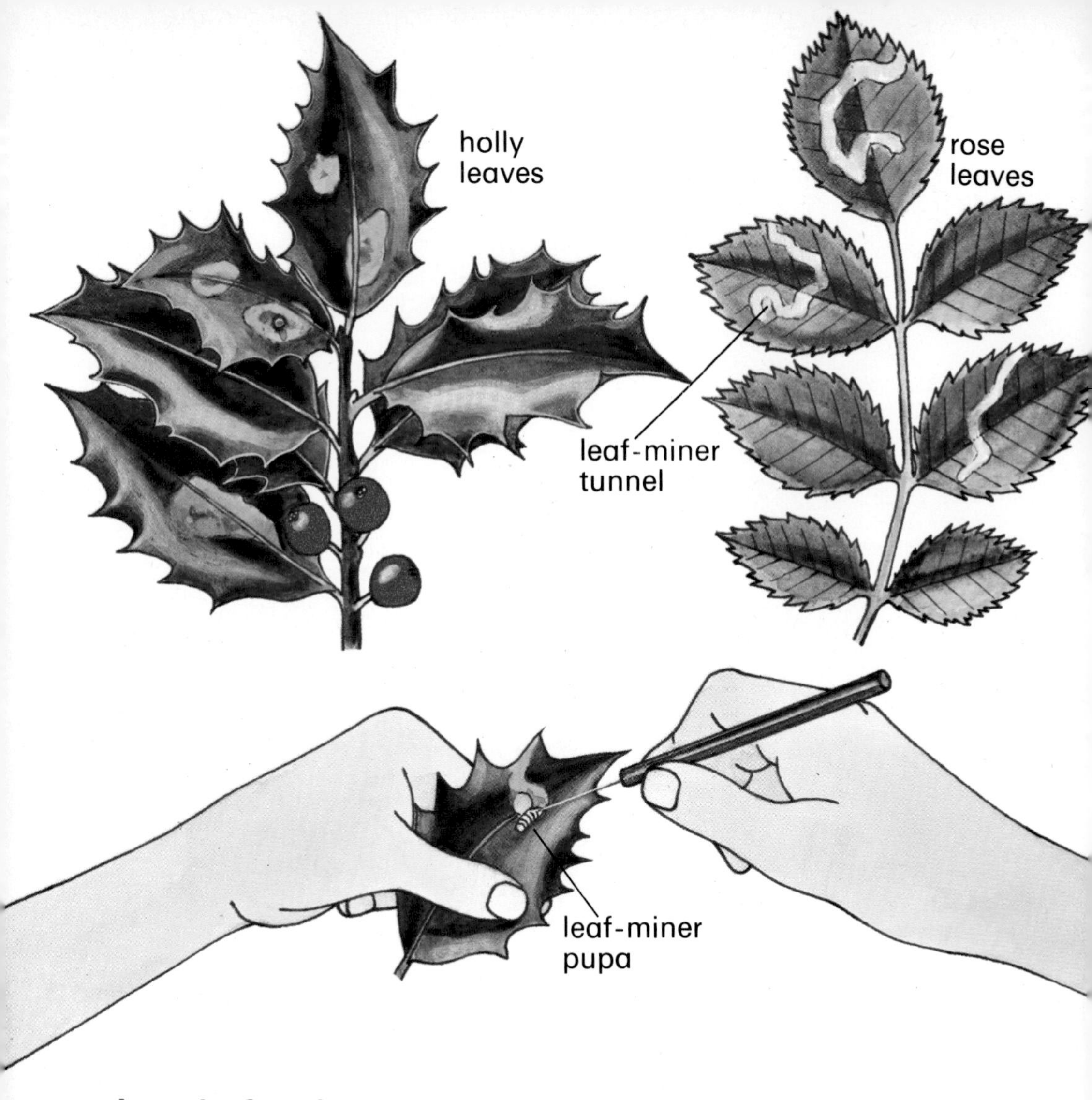
holly
leaves
rose
leaves
leaf-miner
tunnel
leaf-miner
pupa

Look for leaves with marks like these.
The marks show tunnels made by insects called leaf-miners.
Open a tunnel. Can you find a pupa there?

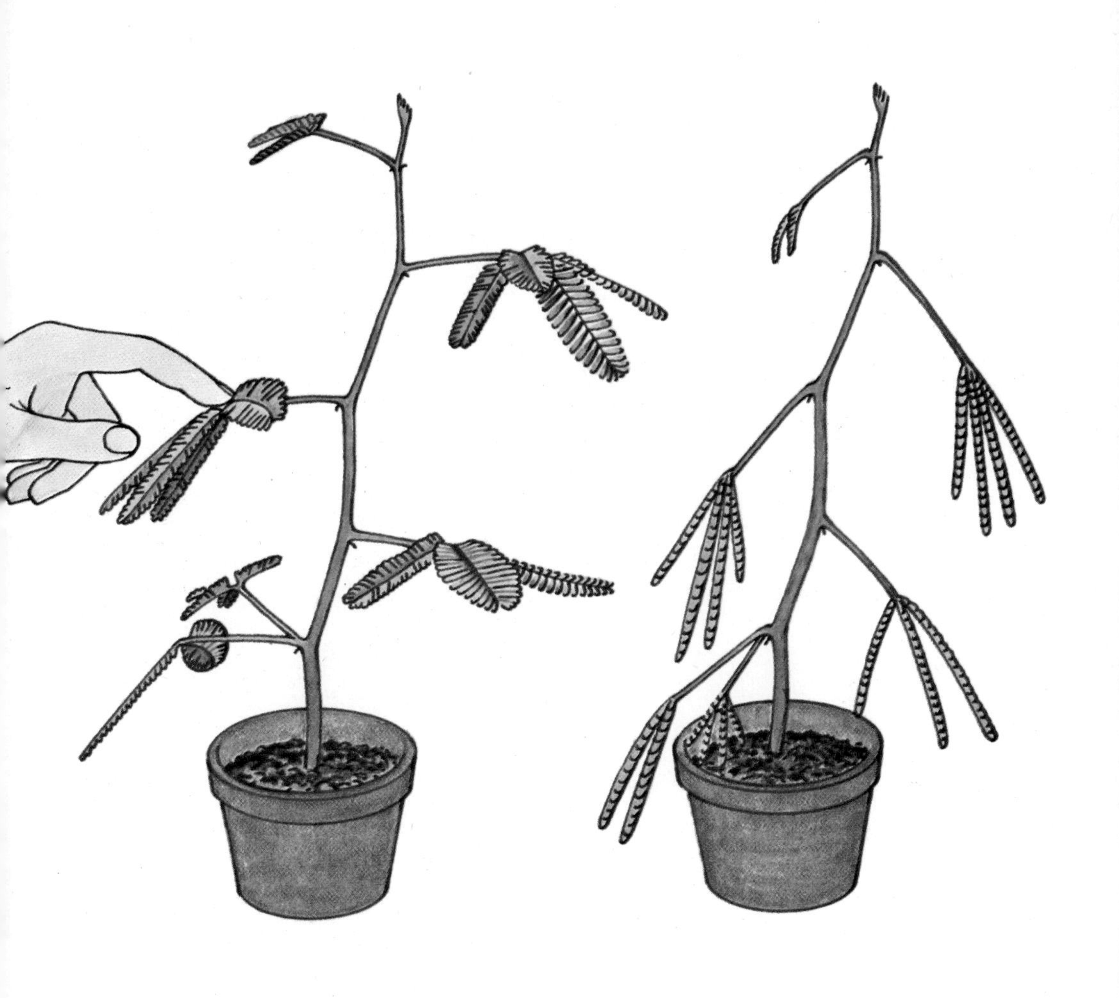

This plant is called the sensitive plant.
When you touch the leaf, it folds up.
Then it slowly opens again.

Index

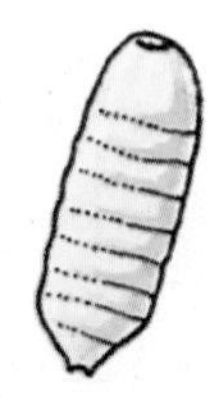